WEST COAST MAIN LINE FREIGHT TRAINS

Jonathan Lewis

AMBERLEY

First published 2018

Amberley Publishing
The Hill, Stroud
Gloucestershire, GL5 4EP

www.amberley-books.com

Copyright © Jonathan Lewis, 2018

The right of Jonathan Lewis to be identified as
the Author of this work has been asserted in
accordance with the Copyrights, Designs and
Patents Act 1988.

ISBN 978 1 4456 7837 5 (print)
ISBN 978 1 4456 7838 2 (ebook)

British Library Cataloguing in Publication Data.
A catalogue record for this book is available from
the British Library.

Origination by Amberley Publishing.
Printed in the UK.

Introduction

The West Coast Main Line is the principal railway route between London, north-west England and Scotland. The last link between London and Glasgow was completed in 1848 by various independent railway companies. The English railway companies soon all became constituent parts of the London & North Western Railway while the Scottish section north of Carlisle remained the Caledonian Railway. In 1923 all these companies were merged into the new London Midland & Scottish Railway. In 1948 all railways in the UK were nationalised as British Railways.

Railways in the nineteenth century were built principally for moving freight as part of the Industrial Revolution. As passenger traffic has become more important, freight has had to fit around an intensive high-speed and local passenger service.

British Railways electrified the route between London and Manchester/Liverpool by 1966, and in 1974 this was extended to Glasgow over the Shap and Beattock summits. Today, freight trains are hauled by a mixture of electric and diesel locomotives. Electric

Still going strong after more than fifty years of service, Class 86s Nos 86610 and 86605 are seen leading the 4M11 Coatbridge–Crewe south through the Clyde Valley on 15 August 2017.

Passing through the scenic Lune Gorge, Class 90s Nos 90045 and 90048 are seen leading the 4S44 Daventry–Coatbridge on 2 September 2017.

Skirting the Lake District mountains, Class 90s Nos 90035 and 90019 are seen leading the 4M25 Mossend–Daventry near Kendal on 25 October 2016.

freight is able to accelerate faster and maintain a higher maximum speed, especially when climbing over the grades of the northern fells. This allows electric-hauled freight significantly faster paths in the timetable as they are not required to let as many faster passenger trains by while they are stationary in passing loops. Faster origin-to-destination times allow rail freight to compete better with road haulage.

With the move towards privatisation, freight trains on the West Coast Main Line are now today operated by all major freight operating companies, which are: DB (formerly DB Schenker and before that EWS); Freightliner; Direct Rail Services (DRS); Colas; and GBRf. The infrastructure is now owned and maintained by government-owned Network Rail.

The Class 86 electric locomotives that can still be seen on freight trains were built for the original electrification from 1965 as mixed-traffic locomotives. The remaining examples are now used solely by Freightliner, hauling intermodal trains.

Class 87s, which were an improved version, were built in 1973 and 1974. These locomotives were mainly used for passenger services until the introduction of the Pendolino trains. Most of this class has now been scrapped or exported to Bulgaria. The photographs of this class in this book were taken during the period when GBRf hired in a number of locomotives to work mail trains.

The Class 90s were built between 1988 and 1990 as mixed-traffic locomotives and have worked on all major electrified lines. Those remaining on the West Coast Main Line today are used on freight by DB and Freightliner for use on intermodal trains. It is common for Class 86 and Class 90 locomotives to work freight trains in pairs.

The Class 92 electric locomotives were built between 1994 and 1996 for cross-Channel freight trains through the Channel Tunnel, but are also used on some trains on the West Coast Main Line. As cross-Channel freight has not developed as forecast, these locomotives have never been used to their full potential. Today, GBRf is the only operator of the class on the West Coast Main Line.

The newest electric locomotives are the Class 88s, which were built in Spain for DRS and introduced into traffic in 2017. These locomotives also have a small diesel engine, allowing them to work away from the wires. So far these locomotives have been introduced into service on intermodal trains between Daventry and Mossend.

The majority of diesel-hauled freight is worked by Class 66s, which were built in North America between 1998 and 2016. All freight operators have Class 66s, which, due to their versatility, operate throughout the country on all types of traffic.

The newest diesel locomotives, the Class 68s, were built in Spain for DRS between 2013 and 2017, and can also be found working on the West Coast Main Line. These locomotives are similar in outline to the Class 88s.

Class 70s were built in the USA between 2008 and 2017. These were originally built for Freightliner but are now also operated by Colas. The Freightliner examples were once common on coal trains on the northern section of the West Coast Main Line, but are now mainly used on intermodal traffic.

As well as these three modern classes of diesel locomotives, some older British Rail-built diesels can sometimes still be found working freight trains, such as the Class 37s, which were built from 1961. In recent years Class 37s have been used by DRS for light trains, including nuclear flask traffic. The most modern British Rail-built locomotive was the Class 60, built between 1989 and 1993 for heavy bulk traffic. The surviving examples work for DB and Colas and can sometimes be seen on the West Coast Main Line.

Freight trains are given a unique four character alphanumeric identification code known as a 'headcode'. The first character indicates the maximum speed of the train. For most trains in this book this is a '4', for a 75 mph freight train, or a '6', for a 60 mph freight train. The second character indicates the area where the train is headed, while the final two characters identify the specific train.

Freight trains move a variety of commodities with a selection of different diesel and electric locomotive types. The principal types of freight moved on the West Coast Main Line are outlined below.

Intermodal traffic makes up the majority of freight traffic on the West Coast Main Line. Intermodal traffic consists of domestic container logistics traffic for companies such as Eddie Stobart, Russell Group and Malcolm Group, including traffic for major supermarkets such as Tesco. There is also shipping container traffic, moving from ports to major cities in the UK.

The 'Enterprise Network' moved wagonload traffic for different customers on a single train between major yards throughout the UK and short trip workings from a yard to a single customer. Trains mainly consisted of MoD and car traffic. At one time timber traffic used to move on the Enterprise Network, moving mainly between Scotland and the wood processing plant at Chirk in the Welsh Borders. Recently, the network has been significantly cut back, and most of the traffic has either ceased or is now moved by dedicated trains.

Coal trains used to make up a significant volume of traffic on the more northern stretches of the West Coast Main Line, moving coal from Scotland to power stations throughout northern England and the Midlands. Coal also used to be moved from the Port of Liverpool to various power stations. When a new 'Coal Tax' was introduced from April 2015, most of this traffic finished; however, some coal trains can still be seen on some stretches of the West Coast Main Line. Biomass is now moved from the Port of Liverpool to Drax power station in Yorkshire, using the West Coast Main Line for some miles around Warrington. Used nuclear fuel rods are moved from all nuclear power stations in the UK to the reprocessing plant at Sellafield on the west coast of Cumbria. Most of these trains use the West Coast Main Line at some point on their journey.

Departmental trains are run for Network Rail civil engineers, carrying track equipment and ballast for engineering possessions across the network. There are regular trains between Network Rail Hub Yards, which make up the 'National Delivery Service'. The yards for the West Coast Main Line include Bescot (Birmingham), Crewe, Carlisle and Mossend (Glasgow).

Another commodity moved on the West Coast Main Line is processed limestone from Hardendale Quarry, near Shap Summit, to the steel works at Port Talbot. Various other short term flows of aggregates are moved on the West Coast Main Line from time to time. China clay is moved once a week between Antwerp in Belgium and Irvine in south-west Scotland using the West Coast Main Line for the majority of its journey in the UK. Various other commodities moved on the West Coast Main Line include metal products and scrap metal, as well as oil.

Mail trains are still run twice a day each way for Royal Mail between Willesden in London, Warrington and Shieldmuir, south of Glasgow, normally using Class 325 electric multiple units. Additional mail trains are operated in the run up to Christmas, and sometimes one of the additional trains has been hauled by a locomotive.

In 2006 Direct Rail Services started running a service for Tesco and Stobart between Daventry and Mossend. No. 66411 was painted in Stobart livery and named *Eddie the Engine* for the service. On 12 April 2007, No. 66411 is seen leading the 4S43 Daventry–Mossend north at Beck Houses, Cumbria.

DBS took over operation of the Tesco train from DRS in 2010, with the traction changing to electric traction using a Class 92. No. 92017 was painted in Stobart livery for the service and named *Bart the Engine*. On 22 June 2010, No. 92017 is seen leading the 4S43 Rugby–Mossend north, crossing the River Clyde at Crawford.

No. 92019 *Wagner*, in its original two-tone grey livery but with an EWS sticker, is seen leading the 4S43 Rugby–Mossend north at Docker on 22 June 2010. During the time EWS operated the train it started at Rugby Yard instead of from Daventry Railfreight terminal a couple of miles to the south.

During 2011 DRS took over operation of the Tesco train again from EWS but hired in Class 92s from EWS so that it continued to be operated by electric traction. Here on 22 August 2011 No. 92019 *Wagner* is seen leading the 4S43 Daventry–Mossend north at Beck Houses.

No. 92030 *Ashford* is seen at Elvanfoot, leading the 4S43 Daventry–Coatbridge north, on 15 October 2012, having just crested Beattock Summit (the highest point on the West Coast Main Line at an elevation of 1,016 feet).

No. 92011 *Handel* is seen leading the 4M48 Mossend–Daventry Tesco train south at Wandel, just north of Abington, on 24 April 2014.

During 2015, DRS stopped hiring in Class 92s from EWS. The train went back to Class 66 haulage, but with a pair of locomotives to keep to the electric timings. On 22 April 2016 Nos 66427 and 66431 are seen leading the 4S43 Daventry–Mossend north at Beck Foot.

On Sunday afternoon the southbound 4M48 working leaves Mossend mid-afternoon instead of in the evening, meaning it is photographable much further south than is normally the case on a weekday. On 17 July 2016, Nos 66434 and 66430 are seen leading the 4M48 Mossend–Daventry south at Hest Bank, between Lancaster and Carnforth.

New Class 68s started to replace the Class 66s on the Tesco train in 2015, becoming the regular traction from the summer of 2016. On 7 July Nos 68004 *Rapid* and 68020 *Reliance* are seen working the 4M48 Mossend–Daventry south at Wandel, just north of Abington in the Upper Clyde Valley.

On 12 October 2016 Nos 68025 *Superb* and 68023 *Achilles* are seen leading the 4S43 Daventry–Mossend north at Beck Houses.

Nos 68003 *Astute* and 68022 *Resolution* are seen leading the 4S43 Daventry–Mossend north, crossing the River Clyde at Crawford, on 24 November 2016.

Nos 68002 *Intrepid* and 68023 *Achilles* are seen leading the 4S43 Daventry–Mossend north at Beck Foot on 24 March 2017.

The new bi-mode electro-diesel Class 88s took over operation of the Tesco train during June 2017 and are able to work the train without double heading. On 12 July 2017 No. 88008 *Ariadne* is seen leading the 4S43 Daventry–Mossend north near Hincaster.

No. 88007 *Electra* is seen leading the 4M48 Mossend–Daventry south at Wandel on 15 August 2017.

No. 88003 *Genesis* is seen leading the 4M48 Mossend–Daventry south at Penrith on Sunday afternoon on 17 September 2017.

During the leaf fall season of 2017, the train reverted to being double-headed due to poor railhead conditions but with Class 88s. On 2 November 2017 Nos 88006 *Juno* and 88003 *Genesis* are seen leading the 4S43 Daventry–Mossend north at Beck Foot.

Nos 88009 *Diana* and 88008 *Ariadne* are seen leading the 4S43 Daventry–Mossend north at Docker Viaduct on 8 November 2017.

In the run up to Christmas in 2017, DRS operated an extra train for Tesco a couple of times a week between Mossend and Daventry. On 16 November 2017 No. 88003 *Genesis* is seen leading the 4Z41 Mossend–Daventry, the extra Christmas Tesco train, south at Greenholme, descending from Shap Summit.

In addition to the Anglo-Scottish Tesco trains, DRS also operates a service from Daventry to Tilbury or Purfleet, beyond the southern end of the West Coast Main Line. On 27 January 2012 No. 66426 is seen leading the 4L48 Daventry–Tilbury south at Chelmscote.

No. 66434 was painted in Malcolm livery by DRS for the contract with Malcolm Logistics that DRS had at the time. It is seen leading the 4L48 Daventry–Tilbury south at Church Brampton on 4 November 2013.

Direct Rail Services started running intermodal trains between Daventry and Scotland for Malcolm Logistics in 2001. On 13 February 2008 No. 66409 is seen leading the 4M44 Mossend–Daventry south at Weston, just south of Crewe.

No. 66425 is seen leading the 4M44 Mossend–Daventry south at Acton Cliffe, between Acton Bridge and Weaver Junction, on 11 November 2010.

No. 66433 is seen leading the 4M44 Mossend–Daventry south at Grendon, Northamptonshire, on 24 February 2011. On this occasion the train is carrying a mix of Russell and Malcolm traffic.

On 24 October 2013 No. 66304 is seen leading the 4M44 Mossend–Daventry south, cresting Shap Summit at an elevation of 915 feet, making it the highest point on the West Coast Main Line in England. No. 66304 is one of the five former Fastline Class 66s DRS took on after Fastline ceased operations.

No. 66434 in Malcolm livery is seen leading the 4M44 Mossend–Daventry south at Beck Foot on 17 December 2013.

During April 2014, DB Schenker took over the contract for Malcolm Logistics from DRS. At first DB Schenker used Class 92s. Here, on 1 September 2014, No. 92024 *J. S. Bach* is seen leading the 4M25 Mossend–Daventry south at Beck Foot.

During 2015, DB Schenker withdrew Class 92s from main line service in the UK (except for the Channel Tunnel and freight on the High Speed 1 line up to London), leading to pairs of Class 90s taking over the trains previously worked by a single Class 92. On 22 April 2016 No. 90024, in Scotrail livery from its days working the Caledonian Sleeper, and No. 90029 are seen working the 4M25 Mossend–Daventry south at Beck Foot.

During 2016, No. 90024 was painted in Malcolm livery to work the service. On 19 June 2016, only a few days after entering service following its repaint from Scotrail livery, Nos 90024 and 90019 are seen leading the 4M25 Mossend–Daventry south at Catterlen, a few miles north of Penrith.

Nos 90024 and 90040 are seen leading the 4M25 Mossend–Daventry south at Beck Foot on 1 November 2016, standing out well with the autumn colours and the Howgill Fells prominent behind.

On a crisp, frosty winter's morning, Nos 90028 and 90037 are seen leading the 4M25 Mossend–Daventry south at Yanwath, just south of Penrith, on 24 November 2016.

Nos 90029 and 90024 are seen leading the 4M25 Mossend–Daventry south at Hartford Junction on 7 February 2017. Between Weaver Junction and Hartford Junction is a particularly busy section of line where freight from Liverpool towards Manchester and the east joins the West Coast Main Line for a few miles.

DBS No. 90034 was painted into a plain DRS livery to go on hire to Virgin West Coast; however, not long after its repaint the remaining loco-hauled passenger set was withdrawn so the loco was returned to DB and given a DB sticker. On 24 March 2017 Nos 90034 and 90037 are seen leading the 4M25 Mossend–Daventry south at Beck Foot.

In addition to the 4M25 Mossend–Daventry, which returns as the 4S47, there is also a daily working from Grangemouth to Daventry, which is at night, apart from on Saturdays, when both workings are in daylight. On 8 April 2017 No. 66118 is seen leading the 4M30 Grangemouth–Daventry south at Shap Beck, climbing up to Shap Summit.

On 2 September 2017 No. 66003 is seen leading the 4S49 Daventry–Grangemouth north through the scenic Lune Gorge, just south of Tebay, on a Saturday afternoon.

There is a Russell Logistics contract for two trains each way per day between Coatbridge and Daventry, which have been operated by EWS, DRS and now Freightliner. On 24 April 2014 No. 66429 is seen leading the 4M82 Coatbridge–Daventry south at Wandel, north of Abington, on the climb up to Beattock Summit.

No. 66433 is seen leading the 4S44 Daventry–Coatbridge north at Greenholme, climbing the 1 in 75 grade up to Shap Summit from Tebay on 16 June 2009. At the front of the train are tank containers carrying sugar for use in the Irn Bru factory. The sugar traffic has now ceased.

Under a threatening evening sky, No. 66426 is seen leading the 4M82 Coatbridge–Daventry south at Wandel, in the Upper Clyde Valley, on 1 September 2014.

Nos 66433 and 66301 are seen double-heading the 4Z10 Coatbridge–Daventry south at Wandel on 4 September 2014.

At the start of 2016 Freightliner took over the operation of the trains for Russell, at first using a mix of Class 66s or Class 70s freed up by declining coal traffic. On 14 July 2016 No. 70002 is seen leading the 4M27 Coatbridge–Daventry south at Scout Green, descending the 1 in 75 grade from Shap Summit.

No. 66529 is seen leading the 4S44 Daventry–Coatbridge north at Greenholme, climbing the 1 in 75 grade up to Shap Summit from Tebay on 19 July 2016.

No. 70003 is seen leading the 4S44 Daventry–Coatbridge north at Southwaite, between Penrith and Carlisle, on 17 September 2016.

No. 66552 is seen leading a very late running 4M34 Coatbridge–Daventry south at Beck Foot on 26 November 2016.

On 2 April 2017 No. 70005 is seen leading the 4M49 Coatbridge–Crewe south at Great Strickland on a Sunday afternoon. The working will be forwarded from Crewe to Daventry on Monday morning.

Freightliner first tried pairs of Class 90s to replace the previous diesel traction in January 2017. However, this was unsuccessful at first due to problems getting them to work together, so the trains reverted back to diesel traction. These problems were fixed by the end of March 2017 and Class 90s took over one of the Russell trains on a permanent basis. On 3 April 2017 Nos 90042 and 90048 are seen leading the 4M27 Coatbridge–Daventry south at Scout Green, descending from Shap Summit.

No. 70005 is seen leading the 4S44 Daventry–Coatbridge north at Shap Wells, nearing the top of the climb up to Shap Summit from Tebay, on 8 April 2017.

By the end of April 2017 both Russell trains were in the hands of Class 90s on a sped-up schedule. On 24 April 2017 Nos 90045 and 90047 are seen leading the 4S44 Daventry–Coatbridge north through the Lune Gorge on the first day of Class 90 traction for this train.

Nos 90043 and 90048 are seen leading the 4M49 Coatbridge–Daventry south at Great Strickland on a Sunday afternoon on 14 May 2017. This working normally runs in the night, but on Sunday it leaves Coatbridge in the early afternoon, giving some different photo opportunities.

Nos 90049 and 90016 are seen leading the 4S44 Daventry–Coatbridge north, climbing up the 1 in 74 grade of Beattock Summit, on 25 May 2017.

Nos 90048 and 90047, both still in the original grey Freightliner livery, are seen leading the 4M27 Coatbridge–Daventry south, passing Oubeck Loop just south of Lancaster on 26 June 2017.

Nos 90048 and 90016 are seen leading the 4M27 Coatbridge–Daventry south at Salterwath, on the start of the descent from Shap Summit to Tebay, on 12 July 2017.

Nos 90042 and 90043 are seen leading the 4S44 Daventry–Coatbridge north at Castle Hill, between Crawford and Abington in the Upper Clyde Valley, on 12 July 2017.

Nos 90042 and 90016 are seen leading the 4S44 Daventry–Coatbridge north in the Lune Gorge on 22 July 2017.

Nos 86638 and 86604 are seen leading the 4M49 Coatbridge–Crewe south at Penrith. This was the first time a pair of Class 86s had worked a Russell train. This was due to a crewing issue on 17 September 2017.

In the run up to Christmas, an extra Russell train normally runs from Daventry to either Coatbridge or Mossend. On 12 October 2016 No. 66548 is seen leading the 4S51 Daventry–Coatbridge north at Beck Houses, climbing Grayrigg bank, north of Oxenholme.

On 2 November 2017 No. 66508 is seen leading the 4S53 Daventry–Mossend extra Russell train north at Beck Foot.

On the southern end of the West Coast Main Line, Freightliner operate services from the Ports of Felixstowe, Tilbury, London Gateway and Southampton to the container terminals of the Midlands and the North. Here, on 27 May 2005, No. 66541 leads the 4M93 Felixstowe–Lawley Street (in Birmingham) north past Carpenders Park.

Nos 86639 and 86627 are seen with the 4L75 Trafford Park–Felixstowe heading south at Watford Junction on 27 May 2005. The 86s will work the train as far as Ipswich where a diesel will take over as the branch to Felixstowe is not electrified.

No. 66578 is seen leading the 4O35 Crewe–Southampton south at the village with a strange name, Cow Roast, just south of Tring, on 21 December 2007.

Unique Class 86/5 No. 86501 was re-geared from an 86/6 to be able to haul intermodal trains by itself, rather than as one of a pair. On this occasion with No. 66556 dead behind, it is seen working the 4M45 Felixstowe–Ditton north at Old Linslade, Buckinghamshire, on 14 May 2014.

No. 90047 is seen leading the 4L89 Coatbridge–Felixstowe south at Old Linslade on 14 May 2014. This is one of the longest freight workings in the UK, which is normally worked by a pair of 86s as far as Crewe, where the traction can change to a Class 90. From Ipswich the train will be worked by a diesel on the final leg of the journey to the Port of Felixstowe.

No. 86501 is seen leading the 4M81 Felixstowe–Ditton Freightliner north at Chelmscote, Buckinghamshire, on 27 January 2012.

No. 90043, named *Freightliner Coatbridge*, the only Freightliner Class 90 to be named, is seen leading the 4L75 Crewe–Tilbury south at Chelmscote on 27 June 2012.

No. 90016 is seen leading the 4L97 Trafford Park–Felixstowe south at Church Brampton on 4 November 2013. No. 90016 was formerly an EWS-owned locomotive, but was acquired by Freightliner as a replacement for fire-damaged No. 90050.

No. 90048 is seen leading the 4M81 Felixstowe–Crewe north at Church Brampton on 17 February 2015. Church Brampton is situated on the Northampton Loop between Milton Keynes and Rugby. Intercity passenger trains use the main line between these points, avoiding Northampton.

Nos 86637 and 86622 are seen leading the 4M54 Tilbury–Crewe north at Church Brampton on 17 February 2015. These are the only two Class 86s painted in the new Freightliner 'Powerhaul' livery.

No. 66535 is seen leading the 4O35 Crewe–Southampton south at Watford Village, south of Rugby, on 1 May 2009.

Unique No. 86501 is seen again, working the 4M88 Felixstowe–Crewe, with No. 70002 dead in train, north at Barby Nortoft on 16 August 2010. The construction of an expansion of Daventry Railfreight terminal can be seen to the left of the train.

No. 90041 is seen leading the 4M87 Felixstowe–Trafford Park north at Grendon, between Tamworth and Lichfield. Unusually, it was running on the fast line on 24 February 2011.

No. 70007 is seen leading the 4L92 Ditton–Felixstowe south at Grendon on 24 February 2011. This working has gone through periods of being worked by Class 66s, 70s, pairs of 86s and 90s in the last decade.

On 21 January 2011 No. 86501 is seen leading the 4M81 Felixstowe–Ditton north at Lichfield. This working was often powered by the unique No. 86501.

Nos 86613 and 86639 are seen leading the 4M87 Felixstowe–Trafford Park north at Searchlight Lane on 26 May 2017. This is on a new section of line around Norton Bridge, which was built so that trains from Stafford to Stoke do not have to cross the fast lines on the flat. All northbound freight now uses the first part of the new line.

No. 90016 is seen leading the 4M81 Felixstowe–Ditton north at Slindon, Staffordshire, on 1 September 2011.

Nos 86612 and 86609 are seen leading the 4M54 Tilbury–Crewe north near Cranberry, Staffordshire, on 26 July 2011.

No. 66566 is seen leading the 4M28 Southampton–Ditton north at Stableford, Staffordshire, on 26 July 2011. Trains from Southampton to the North West generally join the West Coast Main Line at Nuneaton, although some join in London.

No. 86501 is seen leading the 4M81 Felixstowe–Ditton north near Stableford on 2 June 2011. No. 86501 has now been converted back to an 86/6 with its old number of 86608.

On a frosty spring morning, No. 66564 is seen working a poorly loaded 4O86 Crewe–Thamesport south at Stableford on 8 March 2011.

Nos 86604 and 86605 are seen leading the 4L75 Crewe Basford Hall–Felixstowe south at Baldwin's Gate, Staffordshire, on 14 March 2011.

Nos 86622 and 86605 are seen working the 4L92 Ditton–Felixstowe past Weston, just south of Crewe, on 23 October 2007.

No. 90016 is seen working the 4L92 Ditton–Felixstowe south, past Weston, on 7 March 2008.

No. 66577 is seen working the 4M61 Southampton–Trafford Park at Weston on 23 April 2008.

In low November afternoon sun, Nos 86604 and 86638 are seen leading the 4L92 Ditton–Felixstowe south at Acton Grange, between Acton Bridge and Weaver Junction, on 11 November 2010.

On 1 June 2009 Nos 86607 and 86628 are seen working the 4M74 Coatbridge–Crewe south at Red Bank, just north of Winwick Junction, near Newton-le-Willows. No. 86607 was built in 1965 as E3176 at the Vulcan Foundry in Newton-le-Willows, which was a few hundred meters to the left of the photograph.

Nos 86614 and 86639 are seen leading the 4S52 Crewe–Coatbridge north at Beck Houses, climbing Grayrigg Bank between Oxenholme and Lowgill, on 12 April 2007. This working finished soon after this photograph was taken, with the replacement working being re-timed to run in the night.

On 9 July 2017 Nos 90048 and 90043 are seen working the 4M83 Coatbridge–Crewe extra Saturday Freightliner south in the Lune Gorge, south of Tebay, with No. 90042 dead in tow. North of Weaver Junction, Freightliner intermodal trains for Scotland are normally worked by a pair of electric locos due to the grades over the Shap and Beattock summits.

Nos 86613 and 86604 are seen leading an extra 4M83 Coatbridge–Crewe south between Scout Green and Greenholme on 26 November 2016. This additional working sometimes runs on a Saturday if required.

With snow on the ground, Nos 86614 and 86610, nearing the top of the 1 in 125 grade climb of Shap Summit, are seen leading another Saturday additional, the 4M83 Coatbridge–Crewe, past the limestone works at Shap Hardendale on 9 December 2017.

Nos 86637 and 86614 are seen working the 4M74 Coatbridge–Crewe south at Shap Beck, climbing up the grade to Shap Summit from Penrith under a stormy sky, on 8 April 2009. This working currently no longer runs, with the replacement working being re-timed to be at night.

On 22 June 2010 Nos 86639 and 86627 are seen at Greskine, descending the 1 in 74 grade between Beattock Summit and Beattock while leading the 4M74 Coatbridge–Crewe south.

Nos 86627 and 86607 are seen leading the 4M74 Coatbridge–Crewe south, descending from Beattock Summit near Greskine, on 29 May 2015.

In the last moments of glinting sun before sunset, Nos 86610 and 86608 are seen leading the 4L81 Coatbridge–London Gateway south, climbing to Beattock Summit just south of Elvanfoot, on 5 May 2017.

Nos 86638 and 86609 are seen leading the 4M11 Coatbridge–Crewe south at Wandel, just north of Abington in the Clyde Valley, on 12 July 2017.

DRS operated an intermodal working from Ditton to Purfleet, which for a while was worked by Class 37s, giving the class some rare regular long-distance work at the time. On 7 July 2006 Nos 37612 and 37608 are seen leading the 4L46 Ditton–Purfleet past Carpenders Park.

No. 66076 is seen leading the 4G63 Trafford Park–Washwood Heath south at Weston, just south of Crewe, on 13 February 2008. This working was often very poorly loaded.

No. 92007 *Schubert* is seen working the 4H17 Wembley–Trafford Park at Weston on 23 April 2008. The train originated in Europe and operated through the Channel Tunnel. These workings finished in 2009, when DB Schenker stopped using Trafford Park as a freight terminal.

Between 2010 and 2014, DB Schenker ran an intermodal working between Mossend and Hams Hall, near Birmingham. On 22 June 2010 No. 92037 *Sullivan* is seen leading the 4M63 Mossend–Hams Hall south near Crawford in the Upper Clyde Valley. The Class 92 would work the train as far as Bescot, where a Class 66 would take over for the final leg of the journey to Hams Hall.

No. 92041 *Vaughan Williams* is seen leading a poorly loaded 4M63 Mossend–Hams Hall south at Weston, just south of Crewe, on 13 September 2011. Euro Rail Cargo's No. 66071 is dead behind the Class 92. The Euro Rail Cargo Class 66s have been modified for use in France. The train became Fridays-only for a time before finishing completely in 2014.

No. 66132 is seen leading the 4L67 Daventry–London Gateway south at Church Brampton on 17 February 2015. London Gateway, which opened in 2013, is a new deep sea container port and logistics centre on the north bank of the Thames Estuary.

GBRf operate container trains on the southern section of the West Coast Main Line. On 1 February 2012 No. 66719 is seen leading the 4M23 Felixstowe–Hams Hall north at Chelmscote. This locomotive is in Metronet livery from the time when GBRf had a contract with Metronet to run engineering trains on the London Underground.

Between 2006 and 2009, Fastline operated a container train from either Doncaster or Birch Coppice in the Midlands to the Isle of Grain, east of London, using the West Coast Main Line south from Rugby. On 21 August 2006 No. 56303 is seen leading the 4O90 Doncaster–Grain south of Cow Roast, just south of Tring.

For a brief period of time in 2009, Colas Railfreight operated a train for Norfolk Line between Dollands Moor and Hams Hall using hired in Class 56s from Hanson Traction. The train originally came from mainland Europe through the Channel Tunnel. On 27 July 2009 No. 56312 *Artemis* is seen working the 4Z91 Dollands Moor–Hams Hall north at Cow Roast, near Tring.

No. 92001 *Victor Hugo* is seen leading the 6X77 Wembley–Mossend north at Carpenders Park on 25 May 2005. This working conveyed Ford cars from Dagenham and other 'Enterprise' traffic coming from the Channel Tunnel to Scotland. The working finished in 2010, with all traffic being rerouted via Didcot Yard; however, with the closure of Didcot Yard in 2017, the working has restarted, running direct from Dagenham to Mossend.

No. 92030 *Ashford* is seen leading the 6L76 Mossend–Dagenham empty car carrier south at Old Linslade on 14 May 2014. At the time this was an additional train, with the traffic normally going via Didcot Yard.

DBS No. 66114 in the then new DB Schenker livery and No. 92005 *Mozart*, dead behind, are seen leading the 6O15 Mossend–Eastleigh south at Wandel, just north of Abington, on 24 April 2014. On this day the train just consisted of empty car carries for Southampton and Dagenham. A Class 92 would normally lead the train between Mossend and Warrington Arpley Yard.

Nos 90040 and 90018 *The Pride of Bellshill* are seen leading the 6X65 Didcot–Mossend north between Elvanfoot and Crawford in the Upper Clyde Valley on 25 March 2017. On this day the working had tank containers at the front, which were added at Warrington, having originated at Folly Lane, near Runcorn, together with cars behind from Dagenham and Southampton, which were combined at Didcot Yard.

No. 90019 *Multimodal*, with No. 66085 dead behind, is seen working the 6V15 Mossend–Didcot south at Elvanfoot on 25 May 2017. Both locomotives are in the latest version of the DB livery with a larger DB logo and no 'Schenker' branding. At the front of the working on this day are three empty steel rod wagons ahead of the normal empty car wagons.

No. 92029 *Dante*, with No. 37406 *Saltire Society* dead behind, is seen passing Carluke, working the 6M12 Mossend–Carlisle Yard, on 27 October 2005. The working comprises mainly loaded timber heading from Crianlarich in the West Highlands to Chirk Saw Mill, south of Wrexham. At the time these workings were often used to move Class 37s from Scotland where they were allocated to England if they were required. In 2007 Colas won the contract to move the timber traffic to Chirk.

No. 92041 *Vaughan Williams* is seen working the 6O12 Carlisle–Eastleigh, heading south at Greenholme on 16 June 2009. This 'Enterprise' working is entirely made up of VGA vans from MoD Longtown, north of Carlisle, heading to southern MoD bases. The Class 92 would work the train as far as Bescot Yard, where a Class 66 would take over for the remainder of the journey to the South.

No. 37417 *Richard Trevithick* is seen working the 6F42 Blackburn–Warrington south at Winwick Junction on 7 May 2008. This was a trip working from Warrington to collect wallpaper from a factory in Blackburn. The wagons would then be added to a main 'Enterprise' service at Warrington. At the time this was one of the last workings for the declining fleet of EWS Class 37 locomotives. This traffic no longer moves by train.

Another trip working off Warrington is to Folly Lane in Runcorn, carrying tank containers of chemicals. No. 66084 is seen leading the Folly Lane–Warrington working south at Hartford Junction. The working goes to Northwich for the locomotive to run round the train to head back north to Warrington, passing the location again around an hour later in the opposite direction.

A regular car flow operates from Dagenham to Garston. On 14 July 2011 the returning empty working is seen led by No. 92042, with No. 92001 *Victor Hugo* dead behind, working the 6L48 Garston–Dagenham south at Weston, just south of Crewe. This working was often double-headed as a way of moving electrics south from the Electric Maintenance Depot at Crewe.

No. 90036, in its unique grey livery with a yellow roof, and No. 90028 are seen working the 6L48 Garston–Dagenham south at Weston on 13 September 2011. At the time this working was run by a mixture of either Class 90s or Class 92s. GBRf have since taken over the operation of this train and it is now worked either by a Class 66 or Class 92.

A regular flow on the southern portion of the West Coast Main Line is the water train carrying French bottled water to the Midlands. On 21 December 2007 No. 66129 is seen at Cow Roast leading the 6A51 Coventry Prologis Park–Wembley, from where the empty train will be forwarded to France for another load.

During 2010 the working switched to using the Railfreight terminal at Daventry and started being worked by a Class 92 all the way. On 2 December 2011 No. 92015 *D. H. Lawrence* is seen leading the loaded 6B41 Wembley–Daventry north at Chelmscote, near Leighton Buzzard.

No. 92016 is seen leading the 6A42 Daventry–Wembley south at Watford Village on 17 February 2015. During 2015 DB stopped using their fleet of Class 92s on the West Coast Main Line, restricting them to the Channel Tunnel and HS1 trains only, so the working is now in the hands of a Class 66.

Coal trains used to make up a significant proportion of traffic on the northern stretches of the West Coast Main Line until early 2015, when a new 'coal tax' came into force. On 22 April 2011 No. 70010 is seen leading the 6E65 Ravenstruther–Drax loaded coal south at Crawford, in the Upper Clyde Valley. The loadout at Ravenstruther was next to the West Coast Main Line, just north of Carstairs.

No. 66957 is seen leading the 4S34 Carlisle–Killoch empty coal train north at Elvanfoot on 22 June 2010. At that time Freightliner workings for Killoch went north via the West Coast Main Line but returned by means of the Glasgow & South Western line via Dumfries.

Having just crested Beattock Summit, No. 66558 is seen leading the 4S32 York–Ravenstruther empty coal train north on 22 April 2011.

Descending from Beattock Summit to Beattock, No. 66510 is seen leading the 6E65 Ravenstruther–Drax loaded coal south at Greskine on 22 June 2010. At that time the Freightliner workings from Ravenstruther were worked by a mixture of Class 66s and the then new Class 70s.

Coal between Liverpool Bulk Terminal and Fiddlers Ferry power station, west of Warrington, travelled a short distance on the West Coast Main Line between Winwick Junction and Warrington. On 2 May 2011 No. 60049 is seen leading the 6F74 Liverpool Bulk Terminal–Fiddlers Ferry south at Winwick Junction. These workings were normally worked by Class 60s as they could better handle the steep grades out of Liverpool Bulk Terminal.

No. 66519 is seen leading a Saturdays-only 4Z22 Fiddlers Ferry–Crewe empty coal train at Acton Grange, between Weaver Junction and Acton Bridge, on 19 March 2011. The train is returning to Crewe Yard to stable over the weekend.

On hire to Freightliner from DRS, No. 66425 is seen at Weston on 23 April 2008, approaching Crewe while working an empty northbound coal train from Rugeley power station, situated next to the West Coast Main Line.

With mist just clearing early on a summer morning, No. 66520 is seen leading the 6Z02 Liverpool Bulk Terminal–Ratcliffe power station loaded coal at Stableford, Staffordshire, on 23 July 2011.

EWS also moved coal from Scotland to English power stations. On 16 June 2009 No. 66127 is seen at Greenholme, climbing up from Tebay to Shap Summit while leading the 4S04 Warrington–Ayr empty coal train.

On 7 October 2010 DRS moved a rake of former Fastline coal hoppers to Carlisle for use on a trial stone working. Nos 37603 and 37604 are seen leading the 4Z81 Long Marston–Carlisle north at Slindon, Staffordshire.

With coal use declining, some power stations have converted to burning imported biomass. Biomass trains from Liverpool to Drax power station use the West Coast Main Line between Winwick Junction and Hartford Junction. On 8 September 2016 No. 66708 is seen leading the 6E10 Liverpool Bulk Terminal–Drax loaded biomass south at Acton Bridge.

In addition to power station coal trains, coal was also moved from Scotland for use in cement works in England. On 25 October 2016 No. 66013 is seen leading the 6S13 Doncaster Belmont–Killoch empty coal train north at Beck Houses, climbing Grayrigg Bank.

Nuclear flask trains are a common sight on the West Coast Main Line, with Crewe and Carlisle being the hub of operations for flasks on route to Sellafield. No. 37610 *T. S. (Ted) Cassady* and No. 37423 *Spirit of the Lakes* are seen approaching Crewe while leading the 6M63 Bridgwater–Crewe north at Weston on 25 October 2010. The following morning the train will continue its journey to Sellafield.

Nos 37069 and 37259 are seen at Hest Bank, between Lancaster and Carnforth, working the 6K73 Sellafield–Crewe south on 18 July 2016. This working moves empty flasks south from Sellafield to Crewe, where they will go to various nuclear power stations the following day. Flask trains are usually double-headed, with the extra locomotive for backup in case of problems with one of the locomotives.

Nos 37218 and 37609 are seen leading the 6K74 Sellafield–Crewe south at Beck Foot on 8 April 2017. Normally the train would go south from Sellafield on the Cumbrian Coast Line, joining the West Coast Main Line at Carnforth; however, sometimes the working runs north from Sellafield instead, joining the West Coast Main Line just south of Carlisle, as in this instance.

Having just crested Shap Summit, and beginning the steep descent to Tebay, Nos 37259 and 37612 are seen leading the 6K74 Sellafield–Crewe south on 21 January 2017. During 2017 Class 37s were replaced on most flask workings by more modern Class 66s or Class 68s.

No. 37603, with No. 57003 on the rear, is seen working the 6M50 Torness–Carlisle south at Wandel on 7 July 2016. This working runs in top-and-tail formation with a locomotive at each end so it can more easily enter the power station at Torness.

No. 68024 *Centaur*, with No. 68017 *Hornet* attached to the rear, is seen leading the 6M50 Torness–Carlisle south at Elvanfoot on 25 May 2017. The following morning this train will continue from Carlisle to Sellafield.

No. 90028 is seen at Castle Hill, between Crawford and Abington in the Clyde Valley, descending from Beattock Summit while working the 6S50 Carlisle–Millerhill (Edinburgh) on 2 June 2006. At the time this was one of the few EWS Class 90 freight workings, which was making use of the Class 90 that had arrived on the sleeper and was stabled in Edinburgh for the day.

During 2009 the Millerhill to Carlisle and return engineers train started working from Mossend (near Glasgow) instead of Millerhill (Edinburgh), resulting in the traction switching to a Class 92. On 2 April 2010 No. 92031 *The Institute of Logistics and Transport* is seen leading the 4M49 Mossend–Carlisle south at a snowy Abington. No. 92031 was one of only two Class 92s painted in EWS livery, the other being No. 92001.

During 2013 GBRf took over the operation of the Mossend to Carlisle engineers train and used one of its own Class 92s. On 24 April 2014 No. 92032 *IMechE Railway Division* is seen leading the 6S51 Carlisle–Mossend north over the River Clyde at Crawford. These trains are constituent parts of Network Rail's National Delivery Service.

In Caledonian Sleeper livery, No. 92038 is seen leading the 6S51 Carlisle–Mossend north near Elvanfoot, having started the descent down the Clyde Valley from Beattock Summit, on 24 November 2016.

There is a daily, returning engineers train between Crewe and Carlisle. On 7 May 2008 No. 66134 is seen leading the 6K05 Carlisle–Crewe south at Red Bank, near Newton-le-Willows. This train can operate between Carlisle and Farrington Junction (just south of Preston) via the Settle–Carlisle Line.

DRS took over operation of the Crewe to Carlisle and return engineers train in 2013. On 18 July 2017 No. 66429 is seen leading a late 6C02 Crewe–Carlisle north at Beck Foot. The northbound working would normally go through here before dawn.

No. 66423 is seen leading the 6K05 Carlisle–Crewe south at Lowgill, at the south end of the Lune Gorge, with the Howgill Fells behind, on 24 August 2016.

The return Carlisle–Crewe engineers normally leaves Carlisle around noon. On 4 January 2017 No. 66423 is seen leading the 6K05 Carlisle–Crewe south at Beck Foot in some clear winter sunshine.

With snow on the Howgill Fells behind, No. 68023 *Achilles* is seen leading the 6X05 Carlisle–Crewe south at Docker on 23 November 2016. The train is running as 6X05 as opposed to 6K05 as it is carrying point-carrying wagons at the rear, and the X indicates an exceptional load. The train can be operated by either Class 66s or Class 68s. From May 2017 the train was rerouted over the Settle–Carlisle Line on a permanent basis.

In addition to the regular 6C02/6K05 Crewe–Carlisle and return workings, some days there is an additional Carlisle–Crewe and return working. The southbound working is seen at Greenholme on 19 July 2016 with No. 66427 leading the 6K27 Carlisle–Crewe.

Just over a year after the previous photograph, the 6K27 is seen again at Greenholme, this time with a Class 68. No. 68031 is leading the 6K27 Carlisle–Crewe south at Greenholme on 17 August 2017. This locomotive is in the more basic DRS livery to save on adding vinyls as the locomotive will be going on long-term hire to Trans-Pennine Express for passenger duties during 2018.

On 14 July 2016 No. 68022 Resolution and No. 66427 are seen leading the 6K27 Carlisle–Crewe south at Hest Bank. This working continues to use the West Coast Main Line all the way, unlike the 6K05, which now uses the Settle–Carlisle.

There is a daily engineers train from Toton to Crewe that uses the West Coast Main Line between Lichfield and Crewe. On 23 April 2008 No. 66012 is seen working the 6K50 Toton–Crewe, passing Milepost 156 at Weston as it nears its destination.

During 2013 GBRf took over operation of the Toton–Crewe engineers train. On 26 May 2017 No. 66714 *Cromer Lifeboat* and No. 66727 *Maritime One* are seen leading the 6K50 Toton–Crewe north on the new section of line at Searchlight Lane. No. 66727 is in Maritime livery for a contract GBRf has with Maritime Transport.

In addition to the National Delivery Service, engineers trains of ballast also operate between various quarries and 'virtual quarries' where the ballast is stored until it is needed. On 23 August 2011 No. 70010 is seen leading the 6U77 Mountsorrel–Crewe loaded ballast train north at Slindon, Staffordshire. These trains are currently operated by DRS.

Until 2017 a daily ballast train was loaded at Shap Summit for Carlisle. To access the quarry at Shap Summit the empty train from Carlisle had to go via Tebay for the locomotive to run around the train. On 24 October 2013 No. 66423 is seen leading the 6C27 Carlisle–Shap south, passing Shap Summit as it heads for Tebay.

A very unusual combination of No. 37611 and No. 20308 is seen climbing up to Shap Summit at Greenholme, having been to Tebay for the locomotives to run around the train, while leading the 6C27 Carlisle–Shap on 17 December 2013.

On some lines in the Scottish Highlands, Class 37s are the only locomotives allowed due to axle load restrictions, so when a ballast drop is required the trains must be worked by the class. On 23 June 2009 No. 37670 *St Blazey T. & R. S. Depot* is seen working the 6K66 Carlisle–Achnasheen (on the Kyle of Lochalsh line) at Elvanfoot. The locomotive was withdrawn from service soon after this, with DRS Class 37s taking over the work.

Returning to Carlisle from an engineering possession at Mossend, No. 68018 *Vigilant* is seen leading the 6K34 Mossend–Carlisle south at Wamphray, between Beattock and Lockerbie, on 29 October 2017.

Introduced in 2017, the new LORAM Rail Grinders have to be towed long distances by locomotives, normally using a hired-in Class 50 or Class 56. On 16 November 2017 No. 50008 *Thunderer*, with No. 56303 on the rear of the train, is seen leading a late 4Z03 Carlisle–Derby Rail Grinder move south at Docker. The Class 50s were originally built in the late 1960s to work trains on the West Coast Main Line between Crewe and Scotland before the line was electrified, and the locomotives were then moved to the Western Region.

Starting in 2016, limestone began to be moved by Freightliner between Tunstead in the Peak District and the Corus processing plant at Hardendale, just north of Shap Summit. On 2 September 2016 No. 66606 is seen leaving Hardendale, leading the empty wagons on the 6Z51 Hardendale–Barrow Hill. The exchange sidings can be seen in the foreground. The empty wagons are returning to Barrow Hill to stable for the weekend.

No. 66614 *1916 Poppy 2016*, in the newest version of the Freightliner livery, is seen passing Beck Foot while leading the 6H51 Hardendale–Tunstead, returning south empty for another load of limestone on 24 March 2017.

With stone dust blowing from the empty wagons, No. 66621 is seen leading the 6H51 Hardendale–Tunstead south at Docker, with the Howgill Fells behind, on 30 November 2017.

Processed limestone is moved from Hardendale for use in Port Talbot Steel Works in South Wales. On 18 October 2017 No. 66083 is seen climbing Shap Summit at Thrimby Grange while working the 6Z75 Carlisle–Hardendale. The train will be loaded at Hardendale and then run to Margam, near Port Talbot.

Until the closure of Redcar Steel Works, Hardendale also provided limestone for Redcar. On 8 April 2009 No. 66165 is seen working the 6M46 Tees Yard–Hardendale south at Shap Beck on the climb up Shap. The train will be loaded at Hardendale and then go back to Redcar.

Three times a week there is a cement train from Clitheroe, in Lancashire, to Mossend. The working normally uses the Settle–Carlisle Line south of Carlisle. On 11 November 2016 No. 66102 is seen leading the 4M00 Mossend–Clitheroe south at Beck Foot, running via the West Coast Main Line due to the Settle–Carlisle Line being closed by a landslide.

Carlisle receives occasional cement trains from various cement works. On 3 July 2017 No. 66621 is seen leading the 6P62 Carlisle Brunthill–Tunstead south at Shap Beck, climbing up to Shap Summit.

A train not normally seen on the West Coast Main Line is the 6F05 Tunstead–Oakleigh. It is seen here with No. 60071 *Ribblehead Viaduct* at Acton Grange, between Weaver Junction and Acton Bridge, on 30 June 2011. This working was diverted via Manchester and Warrington, travelling on the West Coast Main Line between Winwick Junction and Hartford Junction due to engineering work on its normal route via Altrincham.

An electric locomotive is a rarity on a stone train as they are geared for higher-speed running. However, on 27 July 2016 No. 90040 is seen leading a rake of empty stone hoppers, running as the 6Z94 from Wembley to Carlisle, and passing Hest Bank between Lancaster and Carnforth. This is the only section of the West Coast Main Line to be next to the coast, following Morecambe Bay.

China clay is moved once a week through the Channel Tunnel from Antwerp in Belgium to Irvine in Ayrshire for use in a paper mill. On 22 September 2016 No. 90037 *Spirit of Dagenham* and No. 90035 are seen leading the 6S94 Dollands Moor–Irvine north at Docker, climbing Grayrigg Bank.

From the start of 2017, GBRf took over operation of the train from DB. On the first run for GBRf, No. 92032 *IMechE Railway Division* is seen leading the 6S94 Dollands Moor (originating from Antwerp)–Irvine loaded china clay north at Beck Houses, climbing Grayrigg Bank, on 4 January 2017.

Still in its as-delivered grey livery over twenty years after it was built, No. 92044 *Couperin* is seen leading a late 6S93 Dollands Moor–Irvine north at Greenholme, climbing the 1 in 75 grade up to Shap Summit from Tebay, on 25 January 2017.

No. 92044 *Couperin* is seen again, this time with No. 66737 *Lesia* dead in tow while working the 6S94 Wembley–Irvine north at Beck Foot on 16 August 2017. The Class 66 is used to work the train forward from Carlisle on the non-electrified Glasgow & South Western route via Dumfries to Irvine.

In 2007 Colas Rail Freight took over the operation of all log trains going to Chirk from EWS, which were formerly moved as part of the 'Enterprise' network. Colas had no locomotives of its own at the time, so hired in Class 57s from Virgin Trains or DRS. On 16 June 2009 No. 57308 *Tin Tin* is seen working the 6J37 Carlisle–Chirk south at Greenholme, descending from Shap Summit.

A clean-looking No. 57307 *Lady Penelope* is seen leading the 6J37 Carlisle–Chirk south at Red Bank, just south of Newton-le-Willows, on 7 May 2008. These locomotives were rebuilt from Class 47s and were intended to be used as rescue locomotives in case a train failed on the West Coast Main Line; as such they were fitted with a Dellner Coupling to be able to haul a failed Pendolino if required.

As Colas grew it acquired its own fleet of locomotives, at first using Class 66s, but also older Class 56s for a while. On 24 October 2013 No. 56087 is seen climbing up to Shap Summit from Penrith, at Thrimby Grange, while working the 6J37 Carlisle–Chirk.

No. 56105 is working the returning empty timber train 6V37 Chirk–Carlisle north at Shap Summit on 7 September 2014. On a weekday the northbound train is worked in the middle of the night; however, for a period of time the train that ran south on a Saturday returned in daylight the following Sunday.

Class 60s have now become the normal motive power used for the train. On 5 July 2016 No. 60085 is seen working the 6J37 Carlisle–Chirk out of the loop at Shap Summit. The working often uses the Settle–Carlisle Line, avoiding the West Coast Main Line, between Carlisle and Farrington Junction, just south of Preston; however, at this time the Settle–Carlisle was shut due to a landslide.

No. 60095 is seen approaching Lancaster station while leading the 6J37 Carlisle–Chirk south on 5 April 2017.

Colas have occasionally used their new Class 70s on the train. On 9 August 2017 No. 70804 is seen approaching Lancaster station while leading the 6J37 Carlisle–Chirk. At this time the working was booked via the Settle–Carlisle Line, but used the West Coast Main Line on this day due to a points failure at Farrington Junction.

During 2010 DRS ran a scrap train from Tyne Dock to the metal recycling plant at Sheerness, in Kent. The working was normally worked by a pair of Class 37s and did some roundabout routes. On 17 April 2010 Nos 37667 and 37510 are seen working the 6Z70 Sheerness–Tyne Dock at Chelmscote. On this day the train went north on the West Coast Main Line as far as Rugby, then travelled via Birmingham before running via Burton upon Trent and on to the North East.

Domestic waste is moved on the West Coast Main Line for a short stretch between Hartford Junction and Weaver Junction. These trains originate in Manchester and are moved to an incinerator at Runcorn. On 7 February 2017 No. 66570 is seen leading the 6H35 Runcorn–Northenden south at Hartford Junction.

Aluminium is moved from Europe to Ditton, near Liverpool, for use by Jaguar Land Rover. On 7 February 2017 the first Class 66, No. 66001, in DB livery, is seen working the 6M13 Dollands Moor–Ditton at Hartford Junction. The working will leave the West Coast Main Line in a few miles, at Weaver Junction.

Fuel is moved from Grangemouth Refinery to Dalston, just south-west of Carlisle, on the Cumbrian Coast line. On 4 September 2014 No. 66124 is seen leading the 6S36 Dalston–Grangemouth at Wandel, just north of Abington. The working is now operated by Colas.

Mail trains are run for Royal Mail between Willesden, Warrington and Shieldmuir in Scotland, normally using Class 325 electric multiple units. The trains are currently operated by DBS. On 12 July 2017 No. 325005 and another unit are seen working the 1M03 17.49 Shieldmuir–Warrington mail at Castle Hill in the Upper Clyde Valley. This is the second mail train, which runs south from Shieldmuir in the afternoon and evening.

During the time GBRf had the mail contract, Class 87s were often used to haul the units. On 14 August 2006 No. 87022 *Cock o' the North* is seen working the first southbound mail of the afternoon, the 1M44 Shieldmuir–Warrington, at Castle Hill.

In the run up to Christmas, extra mail trains are operated. On 21 December 2007 No. 87022 *Cock o' the North* is seen working the 1M29 Shieldmuir–Willesden south at Cow Roast. This was one of No. 87022's last workings in the UK before the locomotive was exported to Bulgaria.

In the run up to Christmas in recent years there have been additional mail trains between Shieldmuir and Warrington formed of cargo wagons, which limit the train to 60 mph. On 17 December 2013 No. 90036 is seen leading the 6M02 Shieldmuir–Warrington extra train at Beck Foot.